D1071076

EARTH SCIENCE PROJECTS
for kids

A PROJECT GUIDE TO

EARTH'S WATERS

Christine Petersen

Mitchell Lane

P.O. Box 196
Hockessin, Delaware 19707
Visit us on the web: www.mitchelllane.com
Comments? email us: mitchelllane@mitchelllane.com

A Project Guide to:
Earthquakes • **Earth's Waters**
Rocks and Minerals • The Solar System
Volcanoes • Wind, Weather, and the Atmosphere

Library of Congress
Cataloging-in-Publication Data

Petersen, Christine.
  A project guide to Earth's waters / Christine
Petersen.
     p. cm. — (Earth science projects for kids)
  Includes bibliographical references and
index.
  ISBN 978-1-58415-871-4 (lib. bdg.)
  1. Hydrologic cycle—Juvenile literature.
  2. Water—Juvenile literature. I. Title.
  GB848.P48 2011
  551.48—dc22

                                    2010011150

Printing   1   2   3   4   5   6   7   8   9

                                              PLB

CONTENTS

INTRODUCTION

American philosopher and scientist Loren Eiseley once wrote, "If there is magic on this planet, it is contained in water." Indeed, water is a substance like no other. Covering almost 75 percent of Earth's surface, it helps to control the temperature of our planet and is essential to life. Water makes up approximately 60 percent of the weight of a human body, and without it a person could perish in just a few days. Water can cut through solid rock, yet it has no permanent shape and can therefore take the form of whatever container it fills.

No other substance on Earth can be found naturally in all three phases—solid, liquid, and gas. Water moves freely between these states. Water vapor, a gas, is constantly present in the atmosphere and in soils. As a liquid it is found not only in living things, oceans, and the atmosphere, but also within rocks deep underground. Ice blankets the poles of our planet, also coming and going as snow in winter months. And as a liquid, water is sometimes called a universal solvent because it can dissolve so many other substances. This can be beneficial because water contains nutrients that aid the growth of living things. On the other hand, human health and natural environments may be harmed when water carries pollutants.

Civilizations have risen beside great sources of water, and fallen in its absence. Today our world faces changes in the availability and quality of water.

Water falls to the earth as rain, then flows along rivers to the sea. The sun warms the water, causing much of it to evaporate into the atmosphere, where it gathers and falls again to the earth. This water cycle makes life possible on our planet.

THE WATER CYCLE

Water is constantly moving between the atmosphere, oceans, soils, and living things. This is the water cycle. Water falls as precipitation to Earth's surface. It may fall directly into the ocean, trickle over the surface of the land as runoff, joining rivers and streams, or filter through soils to become groundwater. Plants absorb some of this water through their roots, and many animals take in water by drinking. Both plants and animals give off water during respiration. The sun's heat evaporates water, forming water vapor that rises. The warm air rises into the atmosphere, where conditions are cooler. As water vapor cools it changes state, becoming liquid. Water droplets form around small particles in the air, such as dust, pollen, and salt from sea spray. This process is called condensation. Condensed water forms clouds. Eventually the droplets grow too heavy, and gravity pulls them to earth as precipitation. They may become rain, sleet, hail, or snow depending on air temperature.

The water cycle is hard to imagine, let alone to observe as a whole process. But you can observe some of the steps using a few simple materials found in your home.

MATERIALS

- clean glass jar with lid
- water
- ice cubes
- wooden stick match
- timer
- flashlight

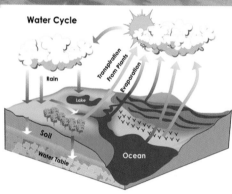

Water Cycle

Transpiration From Plants

Rain

Evaporation

Lake

Soil

Water Table

Ocean

PROCEDURE

This activity involves the use of flames. Be sure to wear safety goggles and keep clothing away from flames. Ask **an adult** to supervise your work.

1. Fill a glass jar with warm water from the faucet. Screw the lid onto the jar. Place the jar on a counter or table. Set a timer for 2 minutes.

2. After the timer goes off, pour most of the water from the jar. A shallow layer, about an inch deep, should cover the bottom.

Cloud formation takes place in the atmosphere, but you can watch it happen by cooling a warm jar of water with ice, then rapidly adding the heat and particles from a blown-out match.

3. Replace the lid, this time turning it upside down atop the jar.
4. Observe the jar for a moment. What do you notice about the water, glass walls of the jar, and lid?
5. Now fill the lid with ice cubes. Set the timer for 10 minutes. Closely observe the jar during this time period. Shine a flashlight through the jar if you need more illumination. Can you see evidence of the water cycle in the jar? Describe or draw these observations in your notebook.
6. After 10 minutes, light a wooden stick match. Lift the lid of the jar just enough to drop the burning match inside.
7. Replace the ice-covered lid immediately. Shine your flashlight through the jar. As in step 5, look for evidence of the water cycle. Did any changes occur in response to the lit match?
8. When these observations are complete, lift the lid of the jar. Inspect the inside of the jar and lid. What has changed since you began the experiment?
9. Use this activity to explain how clouds and precipitation form in the atmosphere.

A desalination pipe draws water from the ocean toward a treatment plant. The water flows through filters that remove larger particles and pollutants. Additional filters strain out salts but allow water molecules to pass through.

DESALINATION

More than 96 percent of the water on Earth is found in the oceans. It contains salts, and many plants and animals thrive in it. Other plants and animals thrive in or consume freshwater, which is replenished during the water cycle. A lot of water evaporates from the oceans. The salts remain behind, so water vapor that enters the atmosphere is fresh, not salty. It falls back to earth as rain, snow, sleet, or hail.

Salt can also be removed from water by desalination. Salt water is heated until it evaporates, and the condensed freshwater is collected. It has been suggested as a way to provide water to those who do not have access to enough of it for drinking, cooking, and hygiene, including those suffering from droughts (long periods without rain).

Opponents are concerned that the large treatment plants used to desalinate water require too much energy. They also point out that the suction from pipes leading into the plants may harm fish and other animals in the ocean nearby. Some feel that it would be wiser for us to learn water conservation—ways to reduce our daily use of water. In parts of the world were water is a desperate issue, small desalination machines might be useful and less damaging to the environment.

MATERIALS

- mixing bowl (or large plastic storage container)
- small bowl or cup
- teaspoon
- measuring cup
- table salt
- plastic wrap
- small weight (for example a marble, rubber bouncy ball, or pebble)

Using simple items from your kitchen, you can desalinate salt water. The resulting freshwater will be drinkable!

For evaporation to begin, your desalination bowl will need to be placed in a window that gets lots of direct sunlight. Make sure that the plastic does not touch the inside bowl. If it does, condensed water will not fall into it.

PROCEDURE

1. Measure one cup of water from the tap and pour it into the mixing bowl.
2. Add 1 teaspoon of table salt. Mix the salt into the water until you can no longer see or feel individual salt crystals.
3. Dip your finger into the water and taste the solution. Make a note about its flavor.
4. Place the small bowl in the center of the mixing bowl, with its open end up.
5. Cover the mixing bowl with a sheet of plastic wrap. The wrap should fit tightly, so no air can enter or exit around the edges of the bowl.
6. Place the bowl near a sunny window.
7. Put a small weight in the center of the plastic wrap. The weight should make the wrap sag over the center of the small bowl—but it should not threaten to rip the plastic or pull it off the larger bowl's edges.
8. Check the apparatus after a few hours. Is there water in the small bowl? If so, taste this water. From where did it come?
9. Use print resources or find reliable Internet sites to learn more about the process of desalination and its potential to solve world water shortages.

In 1989, oil spewed from the Exxon Valdez into Alaska's Prince William Sound, affecting 1,200 miles of coastline. While many substances dissolve in water, oil does not. Oil and water are said to be immiscible (unmixable). When oil spills into the environment, it lies on top of the water, harming the plants and animals that depend on it.

SOLUBILITY

When you have a sore throat, you might use the old medical treatment of gargling salt water. You mix some salt in warm water and swish it around in the back of your throat to make it feel better. In this case, salt is the solute and water is the solvent. Together they form a solution.

The ability of substances to dissolve is called solubility. Water molecules have an electrical charge, and so do salt molecules. They attract each other like magnets, making the salt seem to disappear. But this puzzle-like action does not work with every substance. Pour a small amount of cooking oil into water and the oil will simply float on its surface. This is because oil molecules have no electrical charge and cannot stick to water molecules.

At some point, the solution becomes saturated—it can hold no more of the solute. You can test this with salt and water, then try other solutes for comparison.

MATERIALS

- purified water
- measuring cup
- drinking glass
- teaspoon
- table salt
- metal pie tray
- paper and pencil

- sugar
- baking soda
- cooking oil
- sugar cube or bouillon cube

PROCEDURE

1. Make sure that the purified water is at room temperature. Pour one half cup of it into a drinking glass.
2. Add one teaspoon of salt and stir. Note whether the salt dissolves.

Salt seems to disappear as you stir it into a glass of water. Why isn't the same true of oil? The key is the attraction between salt and water molecules.

A solid solute, such as sugar or salt, will remain behind when the solvent is evaporated. The amount of solute after evaporation is the same as the amount originally added to the solution.

3. If the salt dissolves, repeat step 2. Continue until the salt no longer dissolves. As you add each teaspoon of salt, mark a tally to show the amount you added.

4. Is the salt really still present in the solution? Confirm this by pouring the solution into a metal pie tray. Leave it near a sunny window for a few days. When the water has evaporated, the remaining amount of salt should be the same as the amount you added. Measure it with the teaspoon, and check your tally sheet to be sure.

5. Want to take this experiment further? Try dissolving other solutes. Sugar and baking soda are good solids to test. You can also try cooking oil to see how an insoluble liquid behaves.

6. You can observe the effects of heat as a substance dissolves. Try placing a sugar cube or block of bouillon in cold water. Place another in warm water. Set your timer and see which dissolves faster.

Rainwater and snowmelt can percolate—trickle down—into the ground. There, it can get superheated by underlying hotspots. The vaporized water erupts at the surface as geysers, hot springs, and fumaroles.

GROUNDWATER

Infiltration is an important step in the water cycle. Gravity causes water on Earth's surface to flow downward through the soil. It continues downward until it strikes a solid barrier, or until it reaches a point where the rock is saturated (already filled with water). This point is called the water table. The regions below Earth's surface that hold water are called aquifers. They are not giant underground lakes. Instead, an aquifer is a layer of permeable rock—rock that has air spaces that can hold air and, therefore, water.

Water may be trapped in an aquifer for weeks, years, or centuries. It moves out naturally through springs and other places on Earth's surface where the land dips or breaks to expose the water table. People can also drill into the aquifer and pump water up in wells. By the time water has moved through layers of rock, much of the pollution has often been filtered out. But some chemicals are soluble in water and can remain in groundwater. When this water is obtained from wells, it may be unhealthy for people to drink. Governments carefully monitor the release of chemicals near wells, and drinking water is tested for safety.

MATERIALS

- clear plastic or glass storage container (2 quarts, or 2 liters, is ideal)
- 2 cups small gravel
- 2 cups sand
- paper clip
- paper cup (6- to 8-ounce size)
- spoon
- food coloring
- eyedropper
- wide soda straw
- water

In this experiment, you can observe the movement of water through a model aquifer and see how "pollution" (food coloring) impacts water taken from a well.

PROCEDURE

1. Cover the bottom of a storage container with gravel.
2. Slowly pour sand atop the gravel. The sand will fill the spaces between the gravel but should also form a layer on it.
3. Bend a paper clip to form a straight line. Use one end to poke four or five holes in the bottom of a paper cup. The holes should be made from the inside.
4. Fill the cup with water and hold it over the container. Move the cup over the surface of the container so that all of the sand gets wet.
5. Watch the side of the container. You should be able to see the water percolate through the sand and gravel, forming a layer from the bottom of the container up.
6. Continue to add "rain" on your model aquifer until the gravel is completely saturated. Can you find the water table?
7. Use a spoon to draw a line in the sand dividing the model in half lengthwise.
8. Dig a hole in the sand at one end of the model. Stop when you reach gravel. You can move sand from the hole to the opposite side of the line. Water should flow into the hole from the gravel. You can add more water if necessary, but do not overfill.

This depression is like a lake on land. Because the water table has been exposed, water flows from the ground onto the surface.

9. Now insert the straw into the mound of sand on the other side of the model. Use your eyedropper to draw up water. A well that is drilled into the aquifer works much the same way.

10. Add 2–3 drops of food coloring to the lake.

11. Repeat steps 4 and 9. Do you see any change?

WATER'S FREEZING POINT

Water freezes at 32 degrees Fahrenheit (0 degrees Celsius), right? That's what most of us learn early in our explorations of science. In fact, the story is not quite that simple. People who live next to the ocean often experience air temperatures below this but observe that the ocean does not freeze. This is because salt water has a lower freezing point than freshwater.

As water freezes, molecules bond (stick together) to form crystals—solids built with a repeating molecular pattern. There is more space between the molecules in an ice crystal than in liquid water. Therefore, ice is less dense and will float on water. But molecules of a solute interfere with the formation of crystals. For salt water to freeze, the temperature must be much lower—about −6 degrees Fahrenheit (−21 degrees Celsius). At this temperature, the water becomes saturated with salt. Salt molecules separate from the water, allowing the water molecules to bond and form crystals. Test it for yourself!

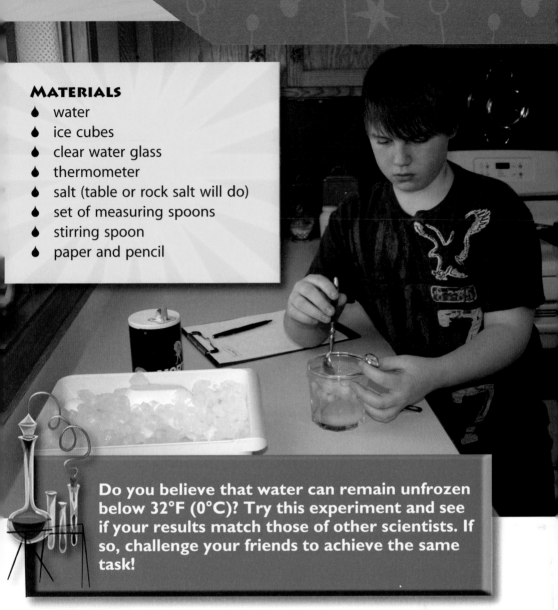

MATERIALS

- water
- ice cubes
- clear water glass
- thermometer
- salt (table or rock salt will do)
- set of measuring spoons
- stirring spoon
- paper and pencil

Do you believe that water can remain unfrozen below 32°F (0°C)? Try this experiment and see if your results match those of other scientists. If so, challenge your friends to achieve the same task!

PROCEDURE

1. Pour water in the glass to fill it halfway.
2. Add just enough ice cubes to cover the surface of the water.
3. Record the temperature of the ice water, and write down your results.
4. Repeat step 2.
5. Add ½ teaspoon of salt to the ice water and stir. Add more ice once the salt has dissolved then record the temperature.
6. Repeat step 5 until the water freezes. What was the final temperature?

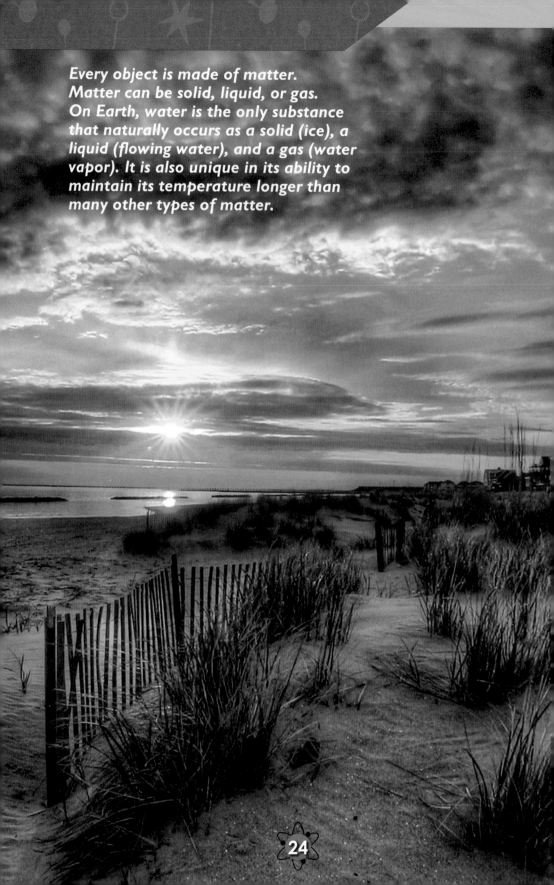

Every object is made of matter.
Matter can be solid, liquid, or gas.
On Earth, water is the only substance
that naturally occurs as a solid (ice), a
liquid (flowing water), and a gas (water
vapor). It is also unique in its ability to
maintain its temperature longer than
many other types of matter.

SPECIFIC HEAT CAPACITY

Why do your feet burn when you walk on the beach, yet a dip in the lake is so refreshingly cool? The answer is a property of matter called specific heat capacity. Every substance absorbs and holds heat differently. You'll notice the same thing when you boil water. A metal pan on the stove will quickly grow hot enough to burn, while the water is slow to boil. But that same pan, when empty, will cool down soon after being moved off the stove. Meanwhile, your hot drink will take a long time to cool. That's because water has a high specific heat capacity—a lot of energy is needed to change its temperature.

This property of water is beneficial to our planet. Water absorbs much of the radiation that enters the atmosphere as sunlight. Regions near the ocean or large lakes experience less dramatic seasonal temperatures than those inland. Because water stores heat, its temperature does not change quickly.

Not sure it's true? You can test this property using soil and water.

MATERIALS

- oven or a sunny spot outside
- two metal cans (coffee or soup cans)
- water
- garden or potting soil
- thermometer (use a scientific or meat thermometer; if possible, obtain two)
- pot holders
- paper and pencil
- clock

PROCEDURE

1. If it's not a warm, sunny day, you'll need to use the oven for this experiment. With **an adult's** supervision, preheat to low—about 150°F.
2. Fill one of two metal cans about halfway with water.
3. Put an equal amount of soil in the other can.
4. Place the two cans in direct sunlight, or in the oven, for two to three hours.
5. Use pot holders to move the cans to a counter. Measure the temperature of the soil and water, making sure that your thermometer touches only the soil or water—not the metal can. Write down the results.
6. Check the temperatures every 20 minutes for two hours, or until they reach the same temperature and do not change. Write down your results each time. What do the data reveal about the abilities of soil and water to hold heat?

The can on the left contains soil. The one on the right holds an equal volume of water. Both were heated to the same temperature in an oven. Which will hold the heat longer?

DENSITY

Density compares the mass of an object or substance to the amount of space it takes up. Some objects are very heavy but small; others are light but large. The density of a given volume of water may vary. Adding solutes increases density. Cold water is denser than hot water because heat makes particles move faster and spread out. (This rule does not apply to ice, however, because of its crystal structure—ice is less dense than water.)

Why is the density of water important in nature? Life in large bodies of water, such as lakes, depends on it. During the cold seasons, air from above cools the surface waters. The cooling water becomes denser and sinks. It pushes lower layers of water out of the way. They rise toward the surface. These layers, in turn, cool down and sink. This process takes months but is continuous over time. It is called turnover.

When organisms die in a lake, they settle to the bottom and are decomposed by bacteria. Decomposition releases nutrients such as nitrogen and phosphorus, which are vital to the growth and survival of other organisms. Turnover pulls some of those nutrients upward, making them available to living things that live near the surface.

Tilt the glass with the salt water. Slowly pour the freshwater down the side of the glass with the salt water.

MATERIALS
- measuring cup
- salt
- red and blue food coloring
- 2 drinking glasses (12 ounces or larger)
- water
- spoon

PROCEDURE
1. Pour a half cup of salt into a drinking glass.
2. Add a third cup of water to the glass.
3. Stir until all of the salt dissolves.
4. Add 2–3 drops of blue food coloring and stir again.
5. Add a third cup of water to a clean glass.
6. Add 2–3 drops of red food coloring. Stir well.
7. Slowly pour the contents of the red water into the first glass. What happens? (The blue-tinted salt water should remain at the bottom of the glass, while the fresh red water rises to the top. Because salt water has a higher density than freshwater, it sinks.)
8. Try this same experiment using warm (red) and cold (blue) water. Slowly pour the cold water into the warm and see what happens!

The cooling towers of nuclear power plants release clean water vapor into the atmosphere. Chemical pollutants bond with water vapor, whether the vapor comes from power plants or natural evaporation. The polluted vapor falls as harmful acid rain.

ACID RAIN

Water's tendency to dissolve other chemicals can create a variety of environmental problems. When fossil fuels are burned in vehicles and factories, carbon dioxide and other gases are released. These gases rise into the atmosphere, where they bond with water molecules.

Scientists use a scale called pH to measure the acidity of water and other liquids. The scale has values from 0 to 14. Lower numbers indicate greater acidity. For example, vinegar is very acidic, with a pH below 3. Pure water has a pH close to 7, which is considered neutral. Bleach is an alkaline, or base, substance, with a pH close to 13.

Rainwater is normally slightly acidic, but polluting gases can bring the pH of rainwater very low. Rain with a pH below 5.6 is called acid rain. It is strong enough to eat away solid rock, and its effect on plants and animals can be severe. Acid rain affects plant leaves, sometimes resulting in widespread damage to forests. It may kill fish, or affect the ability of their eggs to hatch.

There are several ways to test pH. This experiment uses pH test strips, readily available at aquarium and pool stores.

MATERIALS

- three small, clean containers (baby food jars, empty water bottles, etc.)
- vinyl gloves
- pH test strips
- tweezers
- pencil and paper

PROCEDURE

1. Choose several sites from which to obtain water samples. You can pick three points along the length of a stream, test three different lakes, or compare tapwater to bottled water and rainwater.
2. If you collect samples of water in a stream or lake, or use rainwater, put on gloves before taking the sample. Throw the gloves away, and wash your hands when you are done.
3. Hold a pH test strip with tweezers. Dip it into one sample. The manufacturer should offer instructions for how long to immerse the strip and how to read it. Usually the strip needs only a quick dip in the water, and it is compared to a color chart provided with the strips. Write down the numeric result for this sample.
4. Repeat step 3 for your other samples. How do your results compare to each other? If you see significant differences in pH for lakes or streams, contact your local watershed district or pollution control agency. They will welcome your input and may have ideas about how you can help improve the quality of freshwater habitats near your home.

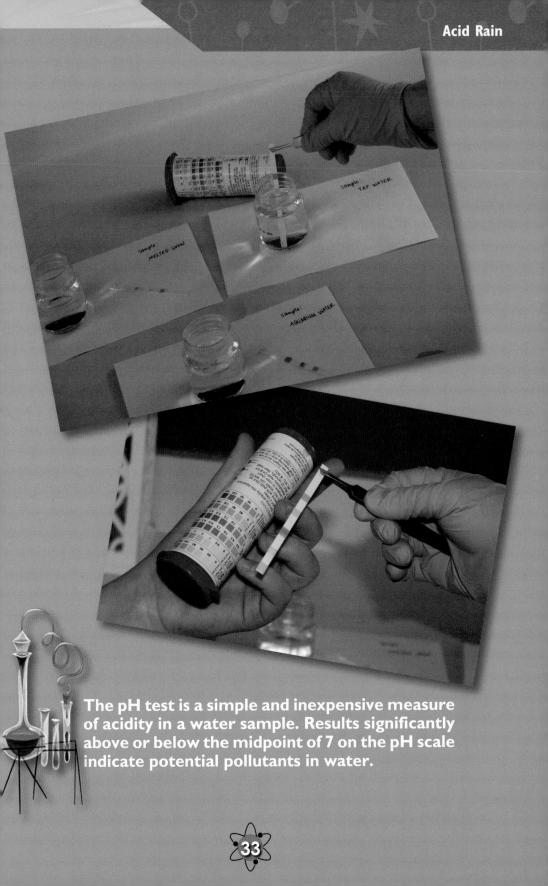

The pH test is a simple and inexpensive measure of acidity in a water sample. Results significantly above or below the midpoint of 7 on the pH scale indicate potential pollutants in water.

A unique property of water is its ability to cling both to itself and to other surfaces.

34

CAPILLARITY

Have you ever noticed water droplets clinging to a window or to your rain jacket? This reveals another property of water—its tendency to stick both to itself and to other surfaces. Cohesion between water molecules forms droplets. It explains how water can flow in streams. Adhesion is the attraction of any liquid to a solid surface. You can also see this when water wicks up a paper towel.

Because of adhesion, water can defy gravity. Plants take advantage of this in their vascular systems. They use roots to draw water from the soil upward into stems and leaves. Water can even move to the top of a redwood tree, more than 300 feet above the ground! This special kind of adhesion is called capillarity. It happens when liquids rise in a tube. Narrower tubes have more surface area on which the liquid can adhere, so the liquid rises higher than it does in wider tubes.

Try these two simple experiments to watch capillarity in action.

MATERIALS: PART ONE

- a small glass bowl or drinking glass
- food coloring
- three glass or plastic tubes of different diameters (straw-sized and smaller)
- plastic tape
- an index card

PROCEDURE: PART ONE

1. Half-fill a glass or bowl with water. Add 2–3 drops of food coloring and stir.
2. Tape the tubes to the index card so that they are evenly spaced and parallel to each other. The thinnest tube should be at one end and the widest at the other.
3. Hold the edge of the index card so that the open ends of the tubes are immersed in the water. Do the tubes fill differently? What does this tell you about capillarity?

MATERIALS: PART TWO
- two tall drinking glasses
- scissors
- measuring cup
- red and blue food coloring
- water
- fresh celery stalk

PROCEDURE: PART TWO

1. Cut the stem of a celery stalk about two-thirds the way up.
2. Pour one cup of water into one glass. Add 2–3 drops of red food coloring.
3. Do the same for the second glass, but use blue food coloring this time.
4. Place the two cups against a wall, and insert each "foot" of the celery stalk into a different glass. You can lean the stalk against the wall to keep it stable.
5. Check the stalk in two days. Use your knowledge of capillarity to explain the results.

Because water does not easily change temperature, it provides a stable environment for many organisms. Living things can be found in rivers, lakes, oceans, and puddles, and even around the hottest volcanic geysers.

LIFE IN THE WATER

A pond, stream, or ocean is much more than a body of water. It contains and supports diverse forms of life. Conditions in the water determine what forms of life can survive there. Is it shady or exposed to direct sunlight? Is the water clear or filled with sediment? How deep is the water, and how fast does it move? Is the water often exposed to pollution from roads, factories, or other sources?

A pond or stream can be an exciting place to begin exploring life in the water. The simplest animals in this environment are called macroinvertebrates. They are often the larvae, or immature life stages, of insects that may later live on land. Dragonfly larvae can often be found in ponds, along with larvae of mosquitoes, midges, and beetles. Snails, clams, worms, and crayfish are other common residents of streams and ponds. Thanks to surface tension, water striders can walk across the top of the water. Some of these animals feed on algae and microscopic green plants in the water. Others are carnivores. In turn, macroinvertebrates are food for frogs and small fish.

You can get to know these mini-creatures in your own local streams and ponds. They may give you clues to the health of that water.

Note: Runoff from streets and parking lots flows into streams and ponds for several days after a rainstorm. Always wait at least three days after a heavy rain to do your sampling to avoid exposure to pollution and pathogens (viruses, bacteria, and organisms that can cause illnesses).

MATERIALS

- wading boots
- vinyl gloves
- bucket
- white ice cube tray
- tweezers
- eyedropper
- spoon
- magnifying glass (at least 10-power)
- paper and pencil
- drift net (fine mesh net with long handle—optional)
- macroinvertebrate identification guide (such as the EPA's Benthic Macroinvertebrates in Our Waters, online at http://www.epa.gov/bioiweb1/html/benthosclean.html)

PROCEDURE

1. Before you enter the stream or pond, put on wading boots and gloves. Do not go into fast-moving water, or water that rises above the boots.
2. Use a bucket to collect a sample of water and mud or sand from the bottom of the stream or pond. If possible, collect a few rocks and add these to the bucket. These are the hiding places of most macroinvertebrates.
3. If you have a drift net, stand in a stream where the water is moving a little. Let the water flow into the open mouth of the net for a minute or so. Then turn the net upside-down in your bucket and clean out the contents.
4. Pick up each rock and examine every surface. Remember that macroinvertebrates may be as little as $1/8$ inch long, and they can be

hard to see! Some look like small worms; others are complex and look something like their adult insect forms.

5. You can attempt to capture them in an eyedropper or spoon. Place macroinvertebrates in the separate sections of an ice cube tray and observe them with a magnifying glass. Be careful not to injure them. Start a collection of drawings, or tally the total number of different macroinvertebrates you find.

6. Macroinvertebrates will also be found in the mud or sand. Use the tweezers to gently probe for them. See if you can find different types from those on the rocks.

7. When you are done, return the creatures, water, and rocks to the stream or pond—preferably to the location where you found them.

8. Try sampling downstream a few miles or in a setting with different conditions than your first site. Does the macroinvertebrate population change?

WATER POWER

Moving water has energy to do work. Running water pushes against Earth's surface, pulling up grains of sediment and moving them through rivers and toward the sea. This energy comes from gravity, which pulls water downstream. Given time, this simple process of weathering and erosion can form deep canyons.

People take advantage of water's energy, as well. Waterwheels have been used for thousands of years. The earliest waterwheels were placed in streams and used to run mills that ground grains or cut lumber. Today, water is an important source of electrical power. Many rivers contain hydroelectric dams that are fitted with turbines, blades that spin in the current. The spinning blades are a kind of wheel, at the center of which is a straight shaft or axle. The axle is connected to a generator, which causes electricity to flow along wires. According to the U.S. Bureau of Reclamation, in 2008 about 6 percent of all electricity used by Americans was produced in hydroelectric plants.*

*U.S. Bureau of Reclamation, "The History of Hydropower Development in the United States," August 12, 2009, http://www.usbr.gov/power/edu/history.html.

MATERIALS

- piece of thick cardboard, approximately 10 inches square
- scissors
- drawing compass (or round object such as a storage container lid)
- scissors
- ruler
- pencil or wooden cooking skewer
- rubber bands
- pan of water
- sink with running water

PROCEDURE

1. Use a drawing compass or round lid to trace a circle on one side of a piece of cardboard. Cut out the circle.
2. Draw two lines that cross in the center of the circle. On each line, cut from the edge of the circle halfway to the center of the circle.
3. Fold these cut sections to form triangular flaps, each pointing the same direction.
4. Push the pencil or skewer carefully through the exact center of the circle. The circle is now a wheel, and the skewer is an axle. Make sure that the wheel can spin on the axis but is not wobbly. You can use rubber bands on each side of the cardboard to hold it in place on the axle.
5. Place a pan of water in a sink. Hold the wheel so that one edge dips into the pan of water. Does the wheel move?
6. Turn on the faucet, and hold the wheel so that water runs over the edge of the wheel. Does it move? Is there a difference in the movement if you flip the wheel and axle around?

Books

Fridell, Ron. *Protecting Earth's Water Supply*. Minneapolis, MN: Lerner Publications, 2009.

Geiger, Beth. *Clean Water*. New York: Flash Point, 2009.

Hollyer, Beatrice. *Our World of Water: Children and Water Around the World*. New York: Henry Holt and Co., 2009.

Sheehan, Thomas F. *Wind and Water at Work: A Book About Change*. Vero Beach, FL: Rourke Publications, 2008.

Strauss, Rochelle. *One Well: The Story of Water on Earth*. Toronto, Ontario: Kids Can Press, 2007.

Sussman, Art. *Dr. Art's Guide to Science: Connecting Atoms, Galaxies, and Everything in Between*. San Francisco: Jossey-Bass, 2006.

On the Internet

Acid Rain Kids Site (from the U.S. Environmental Protection Agency)
http://www.epa.gov/acidrain/education/site_kids/index.htm

The Water Education Foundation
http://www.watereducation.org/doc.asp?id=1022

Water: Kids' Stuff
http://www.epa.gov/ow/kids.html

Water Matters!
http://www.swfwmd.state.fl.us/education/kids/

Water Science for Schools
http://ga.water.usgs.gov/edu/index.html

Works Consulted

Caduto, Michael J. *Pond and Brook: A Guide to Nature in Freshwater Environments*. Lebanon, NH: University Press of New Hampshire, 1985.

Dobson, Clive, and Gregor Gilpin Beck. *Watersheds: A Practical Handbook for Healthy Water*. Toronto: Firefly Books, 1999.

Kandel, Robert. *Water from Heaven: The Story of Water from the Big Bang to the Rise of Civilization*. New York: Columbia University Press, 2003.

Leopold, Luna B. *Water, Rivers and Creeks*. Sausalito, CA: University Science Books, 1997.

Murdoch, Tom, et al. *Streamkeeper's Field Guide: Watershed Inventory and Stream Monitoring Methods*. Everett, WA: Adopt-A-Stream Foundation, 2001.

Suzuki, David, with Amanda McConnell. *The Sacred Balance: Rediscovering Our Place in Nature*. New York: Prometheus Books, 1998.

U.S. Bureau of Reclamation. "The History of Hydropower Development in the United States," August 12, 2009. Retrieved April 26, 2010. http://www.usbr.gov/power/edu/history.html

U.S. Environmental Protection Agency. "Hydroelectricity." Retrieved October 1, 2009.
http://www.epa.gov/RDEE/energy-and-you/affect/hydro.html

U.S. Geological Survey. "Where Is Earth's Water Located?" Retrieved October 29, 2009.
http://ga.water.usgs.gov/edu/earthwherewater.html

World Health Organization. "10 Facts About Water Scarcity." Retrieved October 18, 2009.
http://www.who.int/features/factfiles/water/en/index.html

adhesion (ad-HEE-zhun)—The attraction of a liquid to the surface of a solid.

aquifer (AK-wih-fer)—A layer of rock that holds water.

bond—To stick together; also, the force that holds together atoms in a molecule or molecules in a crystal.

capillarity (kah-pih-LAYR-ih-tee)—The ability of water to rise in a narrow tube.

cohesion (koh-HEE-zhun)—The attraction that makes water molecules stick together.

condensation (kon-den-SAY-shun)—The cooling of a vapor to liquid, such as water in the atmosphere to liquid droplets.

density (DEN-sih-tee)—The mass of an amount of matter compared to its volume (how much space it takes up).

dissolve (dih-ZOLV)—To break up and pass into a solution.

evaporate (ee-VAH-pur-ayt)—To change from a liquid to a gas.

freezing point—The temperature at which a liquid becomes solid.

groundwater—Water trapped in rocks below Earth's surface.

infiltration (in-fil-TRAY-shun)—The movement of water down through soil and rock, caused mainly by gravity.

macroinvertebrate (mak-roh-in-VER-tuh-brit)—One of the small organisms that live in water, such as the early life stages of insects.

molecule (MAH-luh-kyool)—A group of atoms that make up the smallest piece of a substance, so that the substance still keeps all its properties.

pathogen (PATH-oh-jen)—A virus, bacterium, or other microscopic organism that can cause illness.

pH—The measure of hydrogen ions, or acidity, of soil or a liquid.

precipitation (pree-sih-pih-TAY-shun)—Condensed water that falls from the atmosphere as rain, snow, sleet, or hail.

respiration (res-pir-AY-shun)—The act of breathing.

saturated (SAT-chur-ay-ted)—Of a solution, one that is unable to absorb or dissolve any more of a solute; full of moisture.

solute (SAH-loot)—A substance dissolved in another substance.

solvent (SOL-vent)—A substance in which solutes are dissolved.

specific heat capacity—The amount of heat energy it takes to change the temperature of a substance.

water cycle—The ongoing movement of water between Earth's surface, atmosphere, and living things.

ABOUT THE AUTHOR

Christine Petersen is a freelance writer and environmental educator who lives near Minneapolis, Minnesota. A former middle school teacher, she has written more than thirty books for young people that cover a wide range of topics in social studies and science. She has led water quality studies with students, and works with government agencies in her area to monitor and protect rivers and lakes. When she's not writing, she conducts naturalist programs and spends time with her young son.